Sadder and Funday

Andrew Fusek Peters and Polly Peters
Illustrated by Chris Mould

Hodder Children's Books

an division of Hodder Headline Limited

In memory of Marcia Grail 1939-2000
And to our children, Rosalind and Asa
AFP & PP

Text copyright © Andrew Fusek Peters and Polly Peters 2001

Illustrations copyright © Chris Mould 2001

First published in Great Britain in 2001
Reprinted in 2004 by Hodder Children's Books.

The right of Andrew Fusek Peters and Polly Peters
to be identified as the authors and Chris Mould as
the illustrator of this Work has been asserted by them in
accordance with the Copyright, Designs and Patents Act 1988.

All rights reserved. Apart from any use permitted under UK
copyright law, this publication may only be reproduced, stored
or transmitted, in any form, or by any means with prior
permission in writing of the publishers or in the case of
reprographic production in accordance with the terms of
licenses issued by the Copyright Licensing Agency.

A Catalogue record for this book is available from the British
Library.

ISBN 0 340 89439 3

Printed in China

Hodder Children's Books
A division of Hodder Headline Limited
338 Euston Road, London NW1 3BH

CONTENTS

ALL THE FEELINGS IN THE WORLD   5

LOVE
LOVE POEM TO KEVIN
   (HE'D BETTER GET THE MESSAGE!)   6
FIRST LOVE   7
CUSTARD AND KISSING   8
I'M NOT PUDDING UP WITH HIM ANY MORE   9
COUPLES IN COUPLETS   10
PERFECT POSTER BOY   11

FAMILY
SNORING   12
NO MORE HEROES   13
THE MILK CUP   14
MUM   16
DAD   17
AT THE TOP OF THE STAIRS   18
A DAD SONG   20
OUR FAMILY IS IN BAD SHAPE...   21
SEE YOU LATER, ALLIGATOR   22
STEPPING STONES   24
THE TALE OF SALLY SAD   25
IF ONLY THE SCHOOL KNEW THE SCORE   26
IT'S NOT FAIR   28
IT'S NOT FAIR   29
WATCH OUT, HE'S BEHIND YOU!   30

LOSS
E-PET-APH 31
THE RIVER OF TEARS 32
MY CAT SOOTY 33
THE SMILE STEALER 34
WAR STORY 36
GRANDAD 38
NAME CALLING 39

FRIENDS
NO, I'M NOT JEALOUS 40
MAKING AND BREAKING 42
LIP, ZIP, FRIENDSHIP 44
HANGING OUT ON THE NOSHING LINE ... 45
ALL THE SAME 46

BULLYING
STICKS AND STONES 48
BOB THE YOB 50
FIGHT 51
MIS-ADVENTURE 52
BE YOURSELF 53

SCHOOL
PLAYGROUND CHANT 55
NEW SCHOOL 56
THE INSIDER 57
POOLSIDE WARRIORS 58
SCHOOL RHYMES AND SCHOOL TIMES ... 60
MY OWN GOAL! 62
WHAT A JOKE! 63

ALL THE FEELINGS IN THE WORLD

Moanday
Bluesday
Friendsday
Worseday
Cryday
Sadderday
Funday

LOVE POEM TO KEVIN

(HE'D BETTER GET THE MESSAGE!)

Your smile looks like a rip in my jeans,
Your lips resemble an eel,
Your hair has been slurping too much grease,
Can you tell the way that I feel?

Your ears stick up like a pair of forks,
Your hair is greasy spaghetti!
You little squirt of ketchup,
I'd rather SNOG a Yeti!

FIRST LOVE

My head's a boiling kettle,
My heart is a traffic jam
A smile is welded to my face with dimpled rivets.
In class we swap messages like spies,
Ships of paper sailing from desk to desk
Scribbled with felt-tip hearts.
Instant death to those who read them,
Instant trouble if the teacher sees them.
We arrange secret meetings with hand signals
And mysterious flutterings of eyelashes.
After school,
We sneak and skulk down alleyways,
Holding each other's hands as if they were stolen.
We peck in parks and cuddle on swings,
Until the sun gladly, sadly kisses the horizon.
I let go of your fingers and they flutter off like
 sycamore wings.
It's time to go home.
Mum says I look absent-minded. I don't mind.
My mind has moved house, and
I'm head over hills,
Shyly, smiley, highly in love,
So smitten, bitten, this poem's written for you.

CUSTARD AND KISSING

A kiss
is like custard, let me explain:
They both are gloopy, pretty sweet
And make the perfect sloppy treat.
(On the other hand, I must complain,
A smacker from Gran is such a pain!)
But in the end, there's nothing to beat
A kiss.

My heart pours out for Handsome Hussein,
Across the class, when our eyes meet,
I'm a nervous pudding, shuffling my feet,
The Cowardy Custard too scared to gain
A kiss.

I'M NOT PUDDING UP WITH HIM ANY MORE

He thought he was the cream of the brunch,
But now my heart is stuffed with hate,
For Handsome Hussein was out to lunch
(with someone else!)
And I'm leftover on the lonely plate.

I'll admit that I was a trifle upset,
But I didn't mean to create a scene.
Like jelly, my mind (on revenge!) was set
When I saw them ca-noodle in the canteen.

I stuck out my foot, she tripped,
And that was the end of crumbly Katrina.
'I'm sorry, Madeira!' I said as she slipped
And went for a swim in the semolina!
(Ha! Ha! Ha!)

And as for Horrible, Handsome Hussein,
How dare he dump me, little squirt,
I've covered him in custard, let me explain:
You see, he got his Just Dessert!

COUPLES IN COUPLETS

Foster, foment, fan the fire,
Stir the embers, strike, inspire.

Dumbstruck, darling, duck, adore,
Feast your eyes, foot in the door.

Chirrup, chirp, hold jubilee,
Blithely buoyant, brisk as a bee.

Out of humour, in a huff,
Kick up a row and cut up rough.

Blubber, snivel, pipe one's eye,
Wear the willow, weep and cry.

Resent, revenge, retaliate,
Pluck the crow, sing hymn of hate.

Strike the flag, let fighting cease,
Pocket affront and keep the peace.

Meet up, make up, how I miss
Bill and coo and coddling kiss.

PERFECT POSTER BOY

I'm in love with the lad on the wall.
Though as yet, he has not come to call.
I adore him so much, I'm in pain,
Though my longing and waiting's in vain.
I'm his most smitten number-one fan,
And to catch him, I've hatched a great plan:
For without him, I'll always be lonely,
He must know I'm his one and his only.
So I wrote, saying, 'Please, marry me!'
But somehow, it was not meant to be.
His reply said that, 'You can't be mine,
For I'm twenty-two and you're nine!'

FAMILY

SNORING

My brother's snoring
Makes such a sound!
It shakes the bed
And shivers the ground
I never get any sleep,
Not even a peep
Because of that creep...

So I stick my two big toes
Right up his nose!
It's the best way to stop him, I've found!

NO MORE HEROES

My Supermum is extra mad,
When she's been arguing with Dad,
Who's super at ignoring me
For super programs on TV.
My brother's super cruel, he's
Super at the sarky tease,
His super insults snappily
Make me cry unhappily,
And dream of being super cool,
But always I am last at school,
Where hopes of this sad super hero,
Add up to a super zero.

THE MILK CUP

Mum and Dad are united in cheering
Her fancy footwork down the hall.
'Now don't pooh-pooh her, she'll go far.
Our baby's the belle of the (foot)ball!'

At the moment, she's in training,
And when she dribbles, they go dotty.
Her coach (my mum!), she screams with delight,
'The Nappies have lost! Hurrah for the Potty!'

When she throws a skilful tantrum,
It's loud enough to wake the dead!
This is the penalty of having a sister,
The ref blows his whistle, she's sent off (to bed!).

I'm the player they all ignore,
When she's foul, I get the blame
They've chucked me from Division Fun,
Gimme a transfer! I hate this game!

MUM

She's a:

Sadness stealer
Cut-knee healer
Hug-me-tighter
Wrongness righter
Gold-star carer
Chocolate sharer
 (well, sometimes!)

Hamster feeder
Bedtime reader
Great game player
Night-fear slayer
Treat dispenser
Naughty sensor
 (how come she always knows?)

She's my
Never-glum,
Constant-chum
Second-to-none
(We're under her thumb!)
Mum!

DAD

He's a:

Tall-story weaver,
Full-of-fib fever,
Bad-joke teller,
Ten-decibel yeller,
Baggy-clothes wearer,
Pocket-money bearer,
Nightmare banisher,
Hurt-heart vanisher...

Bear hugger,
Biscuit mugger,
Worry squasher,
Noisy nosher,
Lawn mower,
Smile sower...

Football mad,
Fashion sad,
Not half bad,
So glad I had
My
Dad!

AT THE TOP OF THE STAIRS

I live at the top of the stairs,
The safest place to be,
Especially when there's an argument
In my stormy family.

It starts off in the living room,
It isn't very polite,
Their whisper grows into thunder,
I'm glad I'm out of sight.

I hate it when they shout,
It fills me up with gloom,
I hope the hurricane stays below
As I run to the safe of my room.

I think that they forget about me,
And my space at the top of the stairs.
Oh when will the storm blow over?
I wonder if anyone cares?

A DAD SONG

I am empty as a bin bag,
My heart's been chucked away,
Teardrops litter my face,
For Dad has gone away.

My dad, the unjolly postman
Wrote me off like a letter,
I shout and stamp my feet
Will I ever feel any better?

Me and Mum are a pair of clowns
But nobody comes to the show,
Our noses are red with crying,
Why did he have to go?

The door slams like a dustbin lid,
He's gone and it's not right
That I feel like total rubbish,
As Dad's wrapped up by the night.

OUR FAMILY IS IN BAD SHAPE...

MUM ON ONE SIDE

And in between
Me and my brother

DAD ON THE OTHER

They   live   apart

Don't   talk   at all

We   F L Y   between

LIKE A PING PONG BALL

Weekdays with Mum   Dad's in bits
Feels like   we
are   doing   the   splits

ZIGZAG
What a **drag**

Weekdays   weekends
Wish they would   become friends

Piggies in the middle
What about us?

FOREVER CATCHING THE LONELY BUS

SEE YOU LATER, ALLIGATOR

I went to see my dad today.
I didn't want to and clung to my mum like a cat.
My mum hissed, 'hello'. Dad mumbled.
Any moment now she would strike.
Instead, she uncoiled me, and slunk away
through the grass. Phew! No arguments today.
Dad, the awkward flamingo, balanced on one leg.
'How about the zoo? Ooh! Ooh!' he said,
jumping up and down, scratching his armpits.
A smile wriggled on my lips like a fish.
I squirmed about, but was hooked on the idea.
'All right then...'

We trotted around for a while
and came to the apes. I pulled my worst face
at a mountain gorilla.
He paced up and down, up and down,
the way my dad used to in the living room.
The gorilla's eyes were bored and sad.
I looked at Dad. His eyes were far off
in the jungle. I told him I missed him.
Time galloped past as I held his hand.
By the end of the day, I'd seen every animal
under the sun (though it was drizzling),
including a herd of old people
grazing noisily in the cafe.
On the way home, Dad was dog-tired.
He gave me an octopus cuddle
and with a sheepish grin he handed me over
like a gift to my mum.
They stuttered and stumbled goodbyes.
At least they were talking now.

I pressed my nose to the back window
of the car and waved furiously at my dad
as he grew smaller and smaller.
I was a foal, a cub, a gosling gulping down my tears.
He was gone.

STEPPING STONES

Step dad, stew dad,
Cooking-up-a-goo dad.

    Step dad, stop dad!
    Tickle-me-a-lot dad!

Step dad, strop dad,
Caught-me-on-the-hop dad.

    Step dad, still a dad,
    Especially-when-I'm-ill dad.

Step dad, feel glad,
Now I've got a real dad.

THE TALE OF SALLY SAD

When Mum is drinking in the house,
Sally is quieter than a mouse.
Still as a stone on the sofa bed,
Sally fears her mum is dead;
Her bottles are hidden under the sink,
But Mum cannot hide her bad-breath stink.
Sally has never had friends for tea
To see how they live messily.
But worse is when Mum comes to school,
And staggers like a circus fool.
Sally wants to disappear,
But Mum must have her precious beer.
At night beneath the singing breeze
She dreams of happy families.

IF ONLY THE SCHOOL KNEW THE SCORE

Ignore the question, answer back,
I'm a walking, talking flak attack.
Call me Trevor, forever in trouble,
Sent to the Head, every day on the double.

Home alone, Dad's out late
Doing drugs and how I hate
The way he slams against the door,
Ends up mindless on the floor.

Next day in class, I fall asleep,
And homework ends up in a heap.
You wonder why I scream and shout?
I get dealt a daily clout.

Dad hits me until I'm the hard
Bully boy of this school yard.
Trevor, never given a start,
Forever in trouble with a troubled heart.

IT'S NOT FAIR

It's not fair being the oldest,
Mum tells me I have to be 'nice'.
'Set your sister a good example,' she moans.
'I don't have to tell you twice.'
And I have to stay home to look after her,
When I want to be out with my mate.
But instead I am stranded like flotsam,
Stuck playing games that I hate.
She borrows my things without asking,
And copies whatever I do.
Yet if she throws a wobbly,
Then somehow that's my fault too!
Just because she's the youngest,
She ALWAYS gets her own way,
And Mum forever takes her side,
No matter what I try to say.
But most unfair of the whole lot,
The one that gets me in a rage,
Is how come she does all the things,
I was NEVER allowed at her age?

IT'S NOT FAIR

It's not fair being the youngest.
My sister can do as she pleases.
Like boss me about in front of her friends.
And I don't like the way that she teases.
And her bedtime is so much later.
It feels like I always miss out.
Though she claims her evenings are boring.
Which, somehow, I very much doubt.
She's allowed to choose her own clothes.
While Mum is the one who buys mine.
But if I complain they're uncool.
I am told I 'must learn not to whine'.
She makes fun of my taste in music.
And laughs when I dance along.
But I want to be like my sister.
Why does she think that's wrong?
Oh, I know that she thinks I'm just whinging.
Which hardly makes me feel proud.
But she has the freedom to do
All the things that I'm NEVER allowed.

WATCH OUT, HE'S BEHIND YOU!

Oh Mum, don't turn out the light,
For I can't get on with the night!
A woven shadow for his coat,
Thunder screaming in his throat,
He lives in Darkville-Under-Lair,
Has friends who are not even there!
When I flick the bedside light,
I know that he's just out of sight.
Night! You are a crawling creep,
Cut down by the sword of sleep.
Watch out for my deadly yawn,
And my best friend, whose name is... Dawn!

LOSS

E-PET-APH

Gerbil Gerry made a mess
When he got trapped in the trouser press.
It's sad to say, the truth is that
Both of us now feel quite flat.
Poor old pet with a permanent crease,
Gerry Gerbil, Pressed In Peace.

THE RIVER OF TEARS

Why is there rain, and where does it come from, Mum?
And how come clouds live up in the sky?
And why did my brother get ill and die?

The rain is a river of tears, my dear.
For every cloud sees how sad we are here.
Yet I don't know why your brother should die.

Why are the leaves so bright and so green, Mum?
And how do they learn to fall off and fly?
And why did my brother get ill and die?

Leaves are alive and filled with breath, my child.
At the end of the year, they have their death.
But I just don't know how my son could die.

And will he ever come back again, Mum?
And can't we find him if we really try?
And I'm so unhappy, Mum, why did he die?

He's taken a boat to the river of tears
And we shall not see him for so many years
So hold my hand, little one, and wave him goodbye.
So hold my hand tight, little one,
and wave him goodbye.

MY CAT SOOTY

When Sooty died,
I felt flat as a football pitch.
Tears kicked out of my eyes,
Dribbled down my face
Into the mouth,
Scoring an own goal.
All play was suspended.

When Sooty died,
My frown
Was turned down
Like a telephone crying
Brrring-brrring-bring me some happiness.
But nobody answered.

When Sooty died,
My heart was sour as old milk.
I was all bottled up inside,
Remembering a pint of purrs,
Creamy whiskers
And Sooty, pouring herself into my lap.
All my days have now gone off.
And there's no silver-top lining in the cloudy sky.

THE SMILE STEALER

Mum was great at playing jokes,
Pretended her leg was lame
But then the illness stole her strength,
And now it's no longer a game.

She said her head is a boiled egg,
As she laughs off her lack of hair,
'Call me Pirate Peggy!' She smiles,
As she waves her stick in the air.

There's a word no one says in our house,
It's Cancer that's knocked on the door.
Like a lion, I want to pounce,
'There's no one in!' I roar.

Teacher asks about my marks,
And why they are so low,
But I stay silent as the night,
Not wanting my class to know.

My friends just don't understand,
Why I can't play in the park.
I have to put the baby to bed,
And soon it shall be too dark.

Dad is doing really well,
He cooks, he cleans, what a guy.
Looks quite groovy in an apron.
I hope my Mum doesn't die.

The best is when the dinner is done,
And we're comfy in front of TV.
The baby's asleep, Dad's washing up
And my mum is cuddling me.

I bought her an eyebrow pencil,
She's lost every bit of her hair,
Looks like a fading picture,
That needs restoring with care.

One night, I found Dad sobbing,
He turned and he tried to hide,
But I hugged him close as we shared our tears.
You can't hold the crying inside.

I pray, but God doesn't listen.
Perhaps his heart has gone numb.
So all we can do, is to hope and to love
Our peg-leg, boiled-egg Mum.

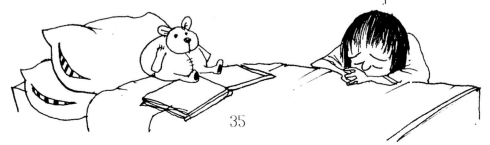

WAR STORY

Mum, I saw the news today
Filled with words of war,
People crying far away,
I can't understand what for?

War is a mountain of hate,
A sad, unconquerable hill,
Why can't they share the view at the top?
But it's cold as they go for the kill...

Mum, I saw the papers today
It said that children were dead,
Were they being very naughty?
Mum, there's a fear in my head.

The young ones are like butterflies
For men with nets of steel,
Who've soldered up their rusting hearts,
And can no longer feel.

 Mum, I heard the radio say
 That mothers were taken away,
 Oh mum don't ever leave me,
 And promise me you'll stay.

Oh, war is a ship of stone, my girl,
Whoever's sails will sink,
A storm is raging in their hearts,
And no one stops to think
That war is a ship of stone my girl
The ocean's bitter drink;
But hold me tight my darling,
We teeter on the brink.

GRANDAD

My grandad in his suit and tie
Looks smart as a button. And I

Lean over to kiss him. He was so old,
His face like a wrinkled leaf now cold.

Perhaps he has gone off to sleep,
Leaving Mum and me to weep.

His soul's a blackbird, watch it fly
Free from his grand old suit and tie.

NAME CALLING

Colour me in with a felt-tip pen;
Find a friend and do it again.
Make me black as a crow's wing tip.
Or shiny brown like an apple seed pip.
Colour me quick or colour me slow,
Paint me pale as newborn snow.
Colour me slow or colour me quick,
Creamy yellow as custard thick.
Every colour has its place,
Runs together in the human race.
Forget those names, remember then
The rainbow in the felt-tip pen.

NO, I'M NOT JEALOUS

No, I'm not jealous, 'cos she won the race,
I'm just naturally red in the face,
And this feeling inside that's boiling away
Is only a kettle I ate yesterday.
And as for the steam drifting out of my ears,
It's an experiment I've worked on for years.
You say that my eyes are flashing fire,
That I want to stick her on a funeral pyre?
Of course not – she's brilliant, she's my favourite friend,
I'd be so (un)happy if she came to a sudden end!
My fists are clenched for practice,
   you must understand
I really want to strangle her,
   oops, I mean... shake her hand!
No I'm not jealous 'cos I got to lose,
And if you believe that, I'll marry my shoes!

MAKING AND BREAKING

Oh Emma is my best friend,
  my best friend,
  my best friend.
Oh Emma is my best friend, the best that there can be.
Until she broke my new pen, my new pen, my new pen.
Until she broke my new pen,
  Now we're not friends you see.

Now Tanya is my best friend,
  my best friend,
  my best friend.
Now Tanya is my best friend, the best that there can be.
Until she beat my test mark, my test mark, my test mark.
Until she beat my best mark,
She can't be better than me!

So Meera is my best friend,
  my best friend,
  my best friend.
So Meera is my best friend, I like her more you see!
Until she spoke to Tanya, to Tanya, to Tanya.
Until she spoke to Tanya,
She can't do that to me!

But now I have no best friend,
  no best friend,
  no best friend,
But now I have no best friend, I'm lonely as can be.
I think I want to make up, to make up, to make up,
I think I want to make up, be friendly with all three.
But will they all forgive me? forgive me? forgive me?
But will they all forgive me?
I've changed, they'll have to see...

LIP, ZIP, FRIENDSHIP

My best mate's turned me into an talkaholic.
Our lips could not zip if you paid them.
In class, our teacher rolls her eyes like a fruit machine,
Trying to keep us quiet.
But words will not do as they are told
And disguise themselves in a whisper
That tiptoes from my mouth to my mate.
This is how we relate.
Clothes and shoes are the subject we study.
We could sit SATs on What to Wear.
In the canteen we catch up,
Lunch on the latest about boys and the box and bands.
My mate, she understands.
When we get home, conversation continues
  on the phone.
Mum goes mad, can't see our need to natter.
Sleepover's the best –
It's an all-night-spout-till-Mum-shouts-out job.
I can tell her anything.
Friendship is a blessing with my best mate.

HANGING OUT ON THE NOSHING LINE

With my best mate,
Secrets fly like a magpie,
Stay safe in the nest of our den.
With my best mate,
We camp out in computer games,
Survive on sweets through all the levels.
With my best mate,
Our bikes cruise cul-de-sac canyons,
Do tricks that make lamposts swoon.
With my best mate,
Scary movies make the living-room twitch,
And shadows gang up on us as we shudder.
With my best mate,
The streets are a palace of pavements
And the chips we dine on, a banquet I share
With my best mate.

ALL THE SAME

Must have, must do
the things that show 'I'm just like you'.
Must like, must be allowed
to prove that I am one of the crowd.
Must buy, must get
every single one of the set.

Must think, must say
I'll only dress a certain way.
Must act, must pretend
I really love the latest trend.
Must love, must be obsessed
with the pop group we think's best.

But why must it be this way?
And who has the final say?
And why must I want these things?
With all the arguments it brings?
I must know, must be aware
it's all about selling the ultimate snare.
I think I'll listen to my own voice,
and have an individual choice.
I must be me, put up a fight,
Just be myself, for it's my right.

BULLYING

STICKS AND STONES

*Sticks and stones may break my bones
But words will never hurt me...*

I whisper it over and over,
To stop my face flaming out my feelings,
But all I can think is
What stupid moron made that up?
Someone who had never met 'her',
She-cat in a leopard-print top.
She prowls the playground with her gang,
With eyes that stalk and stare with scorn,
Ready to pounce with wounding words.
Someone should clip her claws.

She purrs with content at my discontent:
My tears run away like her prey.
I try to ignore the hiss and howl,
Skulk and slink away
From a species filled with spite.

Sticks and stones may break my bones –
Though they would mend
And that's the end –
But words forever haunt me.

BOB THE YOB

'Fat or thin, you won't fit in,
Swot or thick you make me sick.
Black or brown, you've lost this race,
Pink or white, you know your place.
Short or tall, you're in for a fall,
A bit short-sighted, you'll be blighted.
Look at that freckle!' I want to heckle,
'You won't be allowed to be one of the crowd.
Be like me, be like me, it's the only way you see.'
Everyone points at my handsome mug
And says that I am just a thug,
I'm cool as cabbage, strong as stone,
But can't understand why I'm alone.

Now, how do you think the poem ends?
This bully boy has got no friends.

FIGHT

Call me names, no more games, lay your claims,
FIGHT!
Feel a fool, after school, crowd so cruel,
FIGHT!
Lost my mate, heartbeat rate accelerate,
FIGHT!
Pulling hair, just don't care, no 'there, there',
FIGHT!
Flying fist, fall and twist, Ha! You missed!
FIGHT!
Beat the blues, Blag a bruise, both now lose the
FIGHT!
Same old song with gang along, not right but wrong,
FIGHT!
Overdone, setting sun, time to run,
FLIGHT!
Damage deep, wailing weep, will I sleep
TONIGHT?

MIS-ADVENTURE

When I am bullied and hard as hate,
I fly away home to my bed.
It is safe as a bank, my golden books,
Are treasures that fill up my head.

I close the curtains, banish day,
My bedside lamp is a telescope,
That brings to life the hidden words,
Adventure stories filled with hope.

All my heroes have lots of friends,
And dads who share instead of shout;
The baddies never get their way,
But always end up being found out.

Sometimes, there's a furry dog,
Who jumps from the pages to keep me warm,
Safe with my book in my lonely bed,
And outside the raging storm.

I hate to say goodbye to my friends,
Feel sad at the last full stop.
Tomorrow, I go back to school,
Where the bullies come out on top.

BE YOURSELF

She is the
Princess of Put-Downs,
Goddess of Goody-Two-Shoes,
Pop Star of Popularity.

I am the
Sheep of Shyness,
Underling of Ugliness,
Nincompoop of Nerves.

But one day soon, no longer alone,
I shall take up my rightful throne,
The Queen of Confidence I shall be,
The Royal, Regal, Real Me.

SCHOOL

PLAYGROUND CHANT

Lemon, Larch, Laburnum, Lime,
This is the way we work our rhyme.

Chestnut Sweet and Flowering Cherry,
Today I'm mad, tomorrow merry.

Orange, Olive, Old Man Oak,
Give us a kiss and tell us a joke.

Pomegranate, Prickly Pear,
Does he love me, do I dare?

Beech, Bay, Blackthorn, Box,
Cut off all your curly locks.

Almond, Apple, Ash and Alder,
Will I be famous when I'm older?

Wych Elm, Walnut, Weeping Willow,
Lay your head on sleepy pillow

Honeysuckle, Hazel, Hornbeam,
Hop to the dance and hope to dream

Lemon, Larch, Laburnum, Lime,
This is the way we work our rhyme.

NEW SCHOOL

First day.
School gate.
Hope I'm
Not late.
Strange kids.
Fun and play.
I want to
Run away.
So scared.
Want my mum.
When, then
Will she come?
No one
Speaks to me.
Can't wait
'Til half-three.

Boy laughs.
Says Hi!
My smile,
Big as sky!
At break,
Hide and Seek,
Best fun,
All week.
In class,
Dream and draw,
Then play
Some more.
First day.
Yakkety yak.
Can't wait to
Come back!

THE INSIDER

I live at the edge of the playground,
And never get picked for the team,
I'm too shy to join in the games,
I stay in the town of Day-Dream.

I stay in the town of Day-Dream
Far from the noisy playground,
In a tower block of confidence,
Where everyone always pops round.

Everyone always pops round,
I have friends coming out of my ears!
In the town of Day-Dream, the bin-men
Have taken away all my fears.

Now I wake, say farewell to my fears,
Yes, I can join the running around!
And Oh! All the games that we play
In my new found, friendly playground.

POOLSIDE WARRIORS

We march with armoured duffel bags
Into the palace of echoes,
Chasing enemies with a slip-slap
Through long tiled corridors,
Until we come to the dreaded footbath.
Dragons look on with a glare,
As we launch into the air,
Guided missiles with arms and legs:
Crash, splash and the underwater commandos
Trip and topple unwary targets.

Our floats are U-boats
Ambushing the goggle-eyed adults
Who swim up and down, up and down.
Huge slabs of glass are camouflaged with steam.
With fingers, we trace coded messages of
  undying love.
The bell goes off like a bomb,
We brave the obstacle course of
Hot and cold showers,
The torture of towel-flicking,
And the tragic death of terrible jokes.
Now weary warriors,
We retreat through frosty streets,
Our breath unfurling
White as the flag of surrender.

SCHOOL RHYMES AND SCHOOL TIMES

School! Oh! School is a feel-sick-won't-go place,
A stay-at-home-in-case-they-call-me-names-like-Pasty-Face place.

School! Oh! School is a can't-cry place,
A don't-show-your-tears-or-they-laugh-in-your-face place.

School! Oh! School is hate-in-wait-outside-the-class place,
A bully-words-of-sticks-and-stones-to-break-my-bones place.

School! Oh! School is a teacher-tell-me-off place,
A terrible-case! Shoes-unlaced! Hair's-all-over-the-place place.

But,

School! Oh! School is some-days-OK-place,
A best-friend-game-of-hide-and-seek-and-sardines place.

School! Oh! School is a tasty place,
A say-your-grace-yummy-plaice-and-chips-and-peas-
  please-on-Friday place.

School! Oh! School is an out-of-breath-run-and-play place,
A climb-up-grown-up-trees-it's-ace! place

School! Oh! School is and I've-won-first place! place
A best-in-the-race-with-the-fastest-pace-in-the-place place.

Oh! School! Yes! School is a sometimes hot, sometimes
  cold place,
A-Got-to-go, got-to-grow, get-to-know-it's-not-so-bad-
  after-all place.

MY OWN GOAL!

That day I scored the goal that won,
I jumped for joy on to the sun!
My cheeks were flushed, just like the loo
Thank Heaven my aim was perfectly true!
My grin was infectious, (something I ate)
Soon, the surgeons would operate.
My smile so wide, we crossed it by car!
My eyes were twinkling, I must be a star.
On top of the world, my head so big
A forest made a fetching wig!
Shouted and screamed until I grew ho-a-rse,
Then I galloped away (of course!)
Happy as Larry (whoever he may be)
The day that goal was scored by me!

WHAT A JOKE!

Laughed so much, couldn't stop
Got the giggles from the shop!
Creased myself, folded in two,
Split my sides, I need some glue!
Laughed so long it took two weeks
For the tears that streamed across my cheeks
To make a river flow down my face
(we went for a swim and I won the race!)

Yes, that joke was such great fun,
My snot's got shoes on, watch it run!

ABOUT THE AUTHORS

Andrew Fusek Peters and Polly Peters live in an old chapel in Shropshire with two exhausting children, some bored goldfish and a six-toed cat. They have written and edited over 30 books for young people. Anthologies for Hodder Wayland include *The Upside-Down Frown* (a collection of shape poems), *Poems about Seasons*, *Poems about Festivals*, *The Unidentified Frying Omelette* and the bestselling and critically acclaimed teenage collection *Poems with Attitude*:

'...it is rare and welcome to find a collection that speaks so directly to teenagers' - *The Guardian*

'Buy this book and it will be read. I cannot emphasise how much every school needs this. The poems are brilliant.' - *School Librarian*

Find out more about their books on www.tallpoet.com.

ACKNOWLEDGEMENTS

Snoring Broadcast on BBC2's *The Broom Cupboard* 1997 and Radio 4 *Talking Poetry* 1995

The River of Tears Published in *I'm In A Mood Today*, OUP 2000. Broadcast on Radio 4 *Talking Poetry* 1997. Published in *May The Angels Be With Us, Poems of Life, Love, Aids and Death*, Shropshire County Council 1994

School Rhymes and School Times Broadcast on Radio 4 *Talking Poetry*, 1995

New School first published in *Here come the Heebie-Jeebies*, Hodder Wayland 2000

My Cat Sooty, Snoring, The River of Tears, School Rhymes and School Times and *The Milk Cup* all first appeared in *The Moon Is On The Microphone*, Sherbourne Publications, 1997, 2000